34134 00057742 6

WITHDRAWN

Leabharlainn nan Eilean Sia

KU-071-219

J574.92

30675101 J

OOL
ARY
STOCK

Things to do at the Seaside

Paul Humphrey

Photography by Chris Fairclough

WESTERN ISLES
LIBRARIES
30675101)

J574.92

W
FRANKLIN WATTS
LONDON·SYDNEY

First published in 2006 by
Franklin Watts
338 Euston Road
London NW1 3BH

Franklin Watts Australia
Hachette Children's Books
Level 17/207 Kent Street
Sydney NSW 2000

© 2006 Franklin Watts

ISBN: 0 7496 6605 6 (hbk)
ISBN: 0 7496 6855 5 (pbk)

Dewey classification number: 394.26942

All rights reserved. No part of this publication may be
reproduced, stored in a retrieval system, or transmitted
in any form or by any means, electronic, mechanical,
photocopying, recording or otherwise, without the prior
written permission of the copyright owner.

A CIP catalogue record for this book is available
from the British Library.

Planning and production by Discovery Books Limited
Editor: Rachel Tisdale
Designer: Ian Winton
Photography: Chris Fairclough
Series advisors: Diana Bentley MA and Dee Reid MA,
Fellows of Oxford Brookes University

The author, packager and publisher would like to thank
the following people for their participation in this book:
Auriel Austin-Baker; Arrandeep Bola and family; Lucas Tisdale.

Printed in China

Contents

At the seaside   4

Paddling   6

Building a sand castle   8

Rock pools   10

Beach games   12

Picnics   14

Walking on the pier   16

Bouncy castle   18

Merry-go-round   21

Watching the sea   22

Word bank   24

At the seaside

At the seaside, there are lots of things to do.

Paddling

You can paddle
in the sea.

7

Building a sand castle

It takes time to build a big sand castle.

8

Rock pools

You can search the rock pools for sea creatures.

Beach games

It is fun to play with
a bat and ball.

13

Picnics

You can eat a picnic on the beach.

15

Walking on the pier

You can walk along the pier.

Bouncy castle

You can jump on
the bouncy castle...

...or go down the bouncy slide.

20

Merry-go-round

The merry-go-round
will spin
you around.

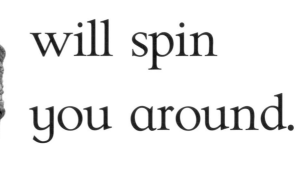

Watching the sea